THE

MOTHER AND HER WORK.

A Child was given to sanctify
A woman — set her in the sight of all
The clear-eyed heavens, a chosen minister
To do their business and lead spirits up
The difficult blue hights. A woman lives,
Not bettered, quickened toward the truth and good
Through being a mother? — then she's none, although
She damps her baby's cheeks by kissing them,
As we kill roses.

E. B. Browning.

And heaven were scarcely heaven
If these lambs which thou hast given
Were to slip out of our keeping and be lost in the
world's ways.

Muloch.

PUBLISHED BY THE
AMERICAN TRACT SOCIETY,
28 CORNHILL, BOSTON.

STEREOTYPED AT THE
BOSTON STEREOTYPE FOUNDRY.

PREFACE.

THE following pages have not been written from any desire for literary notoriety, or from the most distant wish to present in them the example of the author as a model for imitation. But as from time to time, in the prosecution of home duties, her own spiritual perception has been quickened to apprehend the duties and responsibilities bound up in the maternal relation, she has been stirred with an earnest longing that her fellow-laborers in this greatest and noblest sphere of human effort might receive the same impulse.

The greater part of these simple essays were originally prepared by request for the columns of a religious paper; and having in this way been made the medium of profit to many mothers, it is hoped that, by the wider circulation which may be attained in their present form, still more good may be effected. They are now presented to the public, with the fervent prayer that God's Spirit may go with them, and render every truth here uttered palatable and nutritive food to the earnest Christian mother.

Christian mothers, in every rank in life, who, in your own families, or as "missing links" among the households of the poor, are laboring to awaken a deeper interest in the right training of the rising generation, — to you we dedicate and commend this little book.

May each of us who can say, "God knows me and trusts me with a child," though in ourselves utterly insufficient for the achievement of so vast a work, through Him receive such vitalizing power as shall enable us to lift up these immortal spirits to hights of holiness and eternal blessedness.

H. E. B.

CONTENTS.

THE

MOTHER AND HER WORK.

I.

THE MOTHER'S CALLING APPOINTED BY GOD.

A CELEBRATED preacher has remarked, "It is a solemn thing to be married; to have to preach to a congregation from your own blood; to have God put the hand of ordination on you in the birth of your children, and say to you, 'Now art thou a priest unto those whom I have given thee.'" We accept the truth. We recognize it as a fact, that the parent and the pastor alone are honored by receiving their commissions directly from Heaven, since to them are mainly committed the vital interests of the undying soul. The parent, in the family, as in the primary department of the great institution of life, is to prepare men to enter the church militant, where, by pastoral teaching and training, and more active Christian duties, they are graduated into the church triumphant in heaven. We say, to the parent is intrusted this great responsibility; but practically, the commission is given to *the mother*. The father organizes his family, and provides for it. He presides at its head, directs its location and its outward circumstances. The internal arrangements, by far the most important in their moral and eternal bearings, are left for the mother to accomplish. Her silent influence, whatever it may be, constitutes the atmosphere of home. She molds the character and determines the destiny of the succeeding generation. Though the "weaker vessel," yet is she designated by God as the one to whom, in an eminent degree, is intrusted the welfare of the race — the greatest, the most solemn trust ever put into mortal hands.

Within the precincts of home the mother holds this power of projecting character. She may so watch over, screen, guide, and surround her child as to guard it, in a great measure, from evil influences, and bring it more immediately under genial and healthy ones. Or she may so leave it to itself that it will be exposed to indiscriminate, dangerous, and corrupting agencies, which will blight and utterly destroy it. It is the mother alone who has the opportunity to make the first, most delicate, and most enduring impressions on the infant nature. It is to her that the physical and moral training is almost entirely committed. Oh, *does she know* what a work she is called to do, and who has called her to it? Does she know that the great Father has intrusted to her keeping *his own*, that she may have the pleasure, the honor, the peculiar benefit of educating them for him? Does she realize that she is accomplishing an *eternal* work for good or for ill, every day, every hour, yea, every moment when her little one is in her presence? Her looks, her words, her tone of voice, her familiar gestures, her whole carriage and demeanor are fashioning its tastes, opinions, disposition, character — its whole course of life, and its immortal destiny. This is the calling, the work, to which the mother is *appointed* of *Heaven*.

II.

"ENLARGING THE SPHERE."

Women, mothers even, talk of *enlarging their sphere.* And how, we ask, by any possibility, can it be enlarged? They may step out of it into another; but when it embraces the noblest influences of a world, how can it be extended? Has not the mother her hand upon the very springs of being? Has she not the opportunity of molding every living soul upon this broad earth to her own taste and fashion? Take, now, man's acknowledged public superiority, and woman's imperceptible but universal influence, and which, O proud, aspiring, discontented woman, would you choose, for extent or perpetuity? What true woman will not exult in her position? Though hampered, and driven, and cramped by ten thousand whirling, crushing, opposing circumstances, would she exchange her post with any man? Name the man preëminent for intellect, learning, fame, and heroism, and he is but one, and can do but the work of one. But let a mother — electrified with the same aspirations after true greatness, and laying her hand upon the heads of four, six, or eight children — impart the godlike influence to them, and send them forth into the world, and she has, by so many, multiplied her greatness. If she may not send forth men, let her train daughters, who, in their turn, shall transmit the inextinguishable fire of heaven, and she has done more to bless and purify the world than any single individual can possibly accomplish. Talk not of an enlarged and ennobled sphere. It is large and noble enough already. It overwhelms one, who thinks of it at all, with its inconceivable, unutterable vastness. Let us quietly, humbly, hopefully fall back into our retired, unobtrusive place, and patiently labor on, as the coral insects toil to build the beautiful reefs of the Pacific. By and by, what we have builded will rise before the universe in one imposing view; and while angels and men admire, and our Father graciously commends, we will fall and cry, "Not unto us, not unto us, but unto thy name be the glory."

III.

THE MOTHER'S CALLING ONE OF HONOR.

THE mother's is a *most honorable* calling. "What a pity that one so gifted should be so tied down!" remarks a superficial observer, as she looks upon the mother of a young and increasing family. The pale, thin face, and feeble step, bespeaking the multiplied and wearying cares of domestic life, elicit an earnest sympathy from the many, thoughtlessly flitting across her pathway, and the remark passes from mouth to mouth, "How I pity her! What a shame it is! She is completely worn down with so many children."

It may be, however, that this young mother is one who needs and asks no pity.

Stirred with a thrilling sense of the sacred trust reposed in her, serenely conscious of the honor with which God has crowned her, animated with the bright visions of the future, she lives above the ills and disquietudes of her condition. In an atmosphere of love, and peace, and pleasure far beyond the storms and conflicts of this material life, submissive, cheerful, patient, trusting, earnest, she plies her appointed task, and asks commiseration from none. Rather would she be congratulated. "Who would not be a mother?" is the sentiment that swells up from her inmost soul. To be chosen of God as his helper, his co-laborer in the greatest of all earthly enterprises, is no mean favor, no trifling mission. The infinite Creator, in the plenitude of his almighty resources, brings into existence a spirit destined to live for ever. What is this spirit? Who can tell? It is a scintillation from the great, eternal, central light, an emanation from Jehovah's own being, a re-creation of himself, an immortal soul. Of its value God himself has said in impressive interrogation, "What is a man profited if he shall gain the whole world and lose his own soul, or what shall a man give in exchange for his soul?" And this priceless spirit, — so precious that the blood of the Son of God alone could redeem it from impending danger, created on purpose, by our Father above, to add to his own glory and happiness, by swelling the ranks of the pure and joyous spirits that shall forever encircle his throne in heaven, — this never-dying existence, is given, with all its interests, into the hands of a poor, frail, erring, human mother. Hardly does she herself begin to understand the importance of this probationary state in its future and eternal bearings, when, lo, God sends one and another of these new creations, and says to her, "These children I give thee. Take them, and train them for me, and I will pay thee thy wages." What a rare exaltation, what a special distinction, is this!

Mother, has God chosen you in your feebleness and ignorance, as *his agent*, to nurse, cherish, and train *his little ones*, and are you not consciously honored above all others? Are you not raised to the very pinnacle of noble dignity, inaugurated of Heaven to such an office, in such a calling? Will you reject it? Will you throw aside the vestments of office, and come down from your elevation, to dabble in the frivolities of fashion, to partake of ephemeral, unsatisfying, selfish enjoyments? Will you expend your time and chief thought on the external decorations of a body which must soon lie moldering in the dust, instead of being God's minister to prepare souls which he has made to stand happy before him amid the ransomed of heaven, teaching them the songs of the angels and the love-labors of those messengers of light? Will you not rather, with a head bowed under the weight of that crown of glory which God with his own hands has put about it, and a heart prostrate beneath the sense of its utter unworthiness, crying, "What am I, that thou shouldst have chosen me?" say also, "I am thy servant; use me as seemeth good in thy sight"? Most honored of all earth's sinful children is woman; for God has called her to the mother's pains, and toils, and glory! He has delegated her to do *his work!* This privilege, reserved exclusively for her weakness, rewards her pains, elevates her crushed nature, raises her name to an illustrious and everlasting distinction. How painful it is to see those elected to such rank and favor undervalue their privilege, neglect their work, fling aside their waiting laurels, and defile their maternal robes with the dust of earth and self! Can they not, oh, can they not foresee the sacrifice they are making of their own happiness, the wreck of their own joys which awaits them? Can they not hear the solemn voice sounding in their ears, "What wilt thou say when I shall punish thee?"

IV.

THE UNDERVALUED BLESSING.

THE mother of an only child writes thus to a friend: "I write to *congratulate* you, if such a thing be possible, on the birth of your seventh. May you be happy in the accession — I am sure *I* should not be. I can truly say, I am satisfied with my one. I did not marry to be a slave to maternity, to spend my best years in worse than a nursery maid's occupation. My husband does not wish it either. We want to ride, journey, visit, enjoy *ourselves* — and we will not be hindered at every turn by the needs and cries of helpless infancy. We do not wish, either, to spend all our resources in supporting and educating a large family. One is quite enough for us to maintain and care for. So, for economy's sake, as well as our personal convenience and enjoyment, we prefer our condition to yours. Such, in short, are my views about children."

Such "views" need no comment. The weakness and selfishness apparent in every line, the utter disregard of responsibility as a Christian, the ignoring of present duty and future reward, the forgetfulness of womanly nature, — all stamp such a character with a meanness and baseness unworthy of our sex. But is she alone? No, indeed; though we say it reluctantly, yet we are constrained by known facts to acknowledge, that this individual is but the representative of a class, and a large class too. These are not alone gathered from the ranks of worldlings, whose whole avowed aim is self-seeking, but from the ranks of Christ's professed followers, who have publicly ratified the consecration of all they are, and have, and are capable of becoming, to the Lord Jesus Christ.

We have known the young mother to give to the feeble infant in her arms a dose of poison to lull its senses into an unnatural and protracted sleep, that she might join the aimless throng in Broadway, to display a pretty person, or a becoming and fashionable dress. We have seen the nursery forsaken for the ball room, a sick child laid from the fitting pillow of a mother's breast, into the cheerless, uncomfortable crib, for the gay, frivolous chit-chat of heartless visitors. We have known a mother to pass from one scene of indulgence and pleasure to another, and boast that she had not seen her child for days. There are those who have turned from the cold grave which had just opened to receive a moiety of their own being, and secretly congratulated themselves that now they could read their novels, and ride, and walk, and please themselves without interruption. Cold, heartless, cruel woman, unworthy of the hallowed name of mother!

What will be the sentence of such in the day of final account? They have, "for *one morsel of meat*, sold their birthright;" and when afterward they shall desire and seek to inherit the blessing, they will find themselves rejected, with no place of repentance, though it be sought carefully with tears.

V.

THE MOTHER'S CALLING ONE OF TRUST.

THE *sacredness* of the mother's *trust* is still more affecting than her preëminent honor. Were the children nestling around us *ours;* could we do with them as we please, without consulting the wishes or the ultimate designs of another; were we not amenable to another for our dealings with them,—then might we be proud of our name and honor as mothers, and yet totally indifferent to our duties and neglectful of our charge. But no; they are not ours. They belong to our God, and he is waiting till their earthly education be complete, to welcome them again into his home celestial. Oh, what if we should, by fatal mistake, or willful misdeed, or culpable neglect, disappoint his divine expectation, frustrate his design, and doom these souls to irremediable woe, and cause in heaven an eternal vacancy which no other spirits can fill! What if these souls, through our sin, should be *lost — lost!*

The babe in our arms — what is it? An animal to be fed? a fond, darling pet to be caressed? an animate toy to be adorned and admired? We love it — for its very helplessness is winning. Moreover, it is a part of our own being, and the law of our nature impels us to love and care for it. "It is mine," says the mother; "my own;" and she presses the tender nursling to her bosom. How often its celestial workmanship, its inconceivable cost, its priceless value are overlooked! For has it not a soul? Does it not incarnate a germ of immortality? Is it not the hiding-place of a godlike spirit? We lose sight of its ethereal nature by reason of its material covering. We take the casket, and forget the gem; we survey the fashion of the tenement, but overlook the inmate. Perhaps we *never* realize the worth of that which we hold in our close maternal keeping, until it is for ever too late, and the child of our love is buried in irretrievable destruction. Perchance, more fortunate, we may awake from our dreamy indifference before the die is cast; but, ah! the stains, and rust, and canker, which so many years' neglect has suffered to accumulate upon that young heart, can never be entirely effaced. Have we not often seen, will not our own experience testify, what a life-long and tormenting task it is to endeavor to repair the evil results of a misguided education? Many a valuable life has been beclouded and harassed all the way through with clouds and conflicts, the legitimate sequence of parental mistakes and mismanagements. Listen to the moans and cries of distress and sorrow coming to our ears from every side. They are the pitiable bewailings of those rich intellects and noble natures which have been crushed and spoiled by the ignorance or willful sin of those who were set to rear them. Would to God that parents, and especially mothers, might realize the stupendous interests at stake, and looking at their high and holy calling from the standpoint of eternity, so meet their duties that their children should never turn back to reproach and curse their memories! May He give us grace so to order our homes that within the sacred inclosure our little ones may "grow up as willows by the watercourses." Blind and ignorant ourselves, may we receive wisdom from the inexhaustible fountain of Heaven, until we shall know how to lay the foundation upon which they may go on to build characters of symmetry, enduring beauty, sterling worth.

Now we will receive the babe to our arms, and press it to our hearts, with an affection sanctified and sublimated by the thought of what and whose it is. It is, indeed, a precious gem, to be cut and engraved with the signet words of the everlasting covenant, to be read by all worlds, through unending ages, to the praise and glory of our God. It is a stone, quarried by the Almighty, to be made, through our instrumentality, a lively stone for the spiritual house of Christ's church. It is a bark, which we are to provision, man, freight, and propel across the great ocean of time to the shores of eternity. It is a book, whose blank pages are to be written over with our own thoughts and feelings, words and deeds. It is an exotic from a spiritual clime, to be trained with the most rigid care in these ungenial earthly surroundings, that it may be kept from chill and blight, to be restored to the gardens of paradise. It is the power in embryo which shall rule empires, dictate to nations, overturn the world. What mother can tell the future power or influence of that *petite* humanity that lies in swaddling bands before her? Is it a Byron or a Milton? a Nero or a Washington? a Voltaire or a Morrison? But it shall be, mother, *what you make it.* God gives the soul into your keeping; but, with his still, solemn, ever-fixed gaze upon you, is noting all your manner toward it. Is it not a searching thought? Let us look up to that ever-watching Eye, scrutinizing so intently our designs toward his own. Is he *pleased* with our present course? Perhaps he sees that we are careless of our trust, indolent in our duty; or perhaps we misunderstand our work, and will ruin it unwittingly. And to save it, he may stretch forth his hand, and gently remove it from our care. He may deem it best, after all, to do the work himself. Let us not wonder, then, if his messenger, Death, enters our circle, and takes one and another from their earthly sphere. We may feel satisfied that all is right — that the little one is far safer than before. And let us withdraw that longing, earnest gaze after it into heaven, that we may better watch and care for those who remain. Let us labor that when these shall be recalled, they may be found improved and beautified.

VI.

A LEAF FROM THE HEART'S TABLET.

WITH a sacred awe, almost a dread, yet impelled by the strong outgushings of a mother's heart, I approach my child. She is God's child. I may not injure or destroy what belongs to Him, lest I "rob God." And she is so fearfully and wonderfully made,—how dare I, with ignorant hands, touch her? "A harp of thousand strings,"—how can I venture to draw my unpracticed fingers across it? That indwelling spirit, with all its activities, all its tendencies to good and evil,—how shall I manage that? And those warm affections, the out-reaching tendrils of the heart, ever growing, stretching, entwining around something,—how shall I bring for them the true support, and teach them to climb heavenward?

She is destined to develop my Father's image, and I must be the sculptor. How can I bring out form and lineament divine, unless I have the model before me, or the true ideal in my heart? Oh, then, I must have the heavenly pattern shown me before I can do my work. I must study that, mark well each divine feature, appreciate each grace and beauty. O God, I must *know thee* before I can transfer thine image to another!

She is to live for ever, and will always wear the impress of my hand. The workman shall be known for ever by his work. My labor can never be undone. God has put the living material in my hand, and I am to build an eternal destiny. My little one is to me, then, a constant memento of God, of duty, of eternity. Unaided, I must shrink before the vast undertaking. I tremble — I am overwhelmed. I cry aloud, "Who is sufficient for these things?" But a voice, sweet and gentle, whispers in my soul, "My grace is sufficient for thee;" "My strength shall be made perfect in thy weakness." I am reassured. I hope. O God, I give myself to the work.

"I'll do the little I can do,
And leave the rest to Thee."

VII.

THE MOTHER'S COMFORT.

WHAT is home without a baby,
  With each gentle, winning way,
Ever-glancing smiles inviting
  Fond caresses all the day?
Oh, the darling, precious baby, —
  Give her kisses all the day.

Life is dull, and duty pressing;
  Care brings pain and weariness;
But an infant's soft embracing
  Changes all my toil to bliss.
Oh, the baby, clinging baby,
  Like a beam of sunshine is.

How we watch the first vague striving
  After language in her face!
Oh, what yearning love we give her,
  As her tiny steps we trace!
Sure the baby, precious baby,
  Adds to home a sweeter grace.

VIII.

THE MOTHER'S CALLING ONE OF SUFFERING.

THE mother is called of God *to suffer*. We allude not here to her physical sufferings, which we have always been taught to regard as the direct, deserved, and unavoidable curse of Heaven upon the descendants of our tempted, erring mother, Eve, — though these, if rightly considered, may be turned to great account as needed and salutary discipline. But we refer to that continuous series of mental sufferings which she of necessity assumes in behalf of her little ones. "A babe in the house is a wellspring of pleasure," says our "proverbial philosopher;" and the mother's relation is talked of in prose and poetry as one of the most exquisite pleasure. It is all true. No heart so abounds in joy, in gushing tenderness, in fond hope, and the most sacred affection, as that of the mother. And, yet, who that has had the experience of maternity does not know that beneath and around it all — the very substratum of her life — the element which nourishes these delicious joys into growth and efflorescence is *suffering*, sacrifice, toil, and trial? We speak of the *true mother;* not of the vain, foolish, wicked woman who receives her little one at the hands of its Creator with reluctance and dissatisfaction, to complain of it as a burden, an annoying and wearying care, to tear it away from its helpless clingings, and leave it, solitary and unsoothed, to suffer, and perchance to die, that she who gave it birth may busily ply every means of gratifying her own selfishness at the fount of worldly pleasure.

But the *true mother* yields herself uncomplainingly, yea, cheerfully, to the wholesome privation, solitude, and self-denial allotted her. She no longer lives for herself, but gives her life to nourish up the little one intrusted to her keeping; and as one after another the birdlings crowd into the home-nest, with each one a new life seems given to her, that all may share alike in her affectionate care and solicitude. Every favorite pursuit, taste, and inclination, however dear, incompatible with her maternal duties, is relinquished. Was she fond of traveling — of visiting the wonderful in nature and in art, of mingling in new and often-varying scenes? Now she has found "an abiding city," and no allurements are strong enough to tempt her thence. Had society charms for her, and in the social circle and the festive throng were her chief delights? Now she stays at home, and the gorgeous saloon and brilliant assemblage give place to the nursery and the baby. Was she devoted to literary pursuits? Now the library is seldom visited, the cherished studies are neglected, the rattle and the doll are substituted for the pen. Her piano is silent, while she chants softly and sweetly the soothing lullaby. Her dress can last another season now, and the hat — oh, she does not care if it is not in the latest mode, for she has a baby to look after, and has no time for herself. Even the ride and the walk are given up, perhaps too often, with the excuse, "Baby-tending is exercise enough for me." Her whole life is reversed. "She seems not the same being," says one, "to stoop from such a course as hers has been, of high, intellectual, refined pursuits, to become so absorbed with the petty occupations and wailing weaknesses of infancy." But do you not understand? She is executing a heaven-drawn commission: "To the weak she becomes as weak, that she may gain the weak." She lays down her life, that the young life rooted in it may grow up to a perfect and blessed maturity. She wraps herself in the robes of infantile simplicity, and, burying her womanly nature in the tomb of childhood, patiently awaits the sure-coming resurrection in the form of a noble, high-minded, world-stirring son, or a virtuous, lovely daughter. The nursery is the mother's chrysalis. Let her abide for a little season, and she shall emerge triumphantly, with ethereal wings and a happy flight.

Yet she *suffers* in all this. It can not be otherwise. Were she to consult her own inclinations, her personal feelings, she would not submit to all these self-denials; she would indulge herself in far different pursuits. Were it not for the "joy set before her," she *would not* "endure the cross, despising the shame." Her daily life is a constant sacrificing of self, an hourly crucifixion of her own cherished wishes. She loves quiet better than the noise and confusion of romping, uproarious childhood. She would rather read than tell stories, the wee baby stories, that must be told over, and over, and over again to the untiring ear of interested little ones. She would like to be at the piano, or the guitar, with sweet melodies to soothe and comfort herself; but she must not, for the little prattler at her side, or on her knee, wants mamma to sing "chick-a-dee-dee," or "bob-o-linkum," for the hundred and fiftieth time. She is weary, but she must not rest yet. "Wait until the children are all sweetly sleeping," Affection whispers. It is done — and in the evening she seats herself by the side of her husband, to rest and refresh herself in pleasant converse for the morrow, when, lo! a wailing cry of sudden sickness comes through the half-open door, and again she starts to add a night's watching and feverish anxiety to the day's toil.

How hard it is for the fond, loving mother to deny the many beseechings of impetuous and misjudging childhood, when it asks for what would only cause it harm! It does not, can not, understand why the indulgence it so much craves should be injurious. And as our tender Father "pities his children," and "grieves them not willingly," so she denies her child with sorrow and with tears. Perverse and wayward infancy must also be disciplined. How often would her soul "spare for its crying"! How is she punished tenfold in punishing her child! But love — love which overlooks the present trial, fixing its steadfast gaze on the glorious finale — impels her to the work. And days, and weeks, and years of such patient care, unceasing sacrifice, unmitigated toil, must she pass through; yea, with heart-struggles, scalding tears, importunate pleadings, unknown to all but the Eternal, before her work is done. Blessed, thrice blessed are they who can look back upon the arduous task *well* achieved.

And other sorrow comes — long, anxious watchings by the bed of sickness and pain. How hard it is to see a little one laid low by wasting disease — tossed with fever, wild with delirium, tortured by distress which it can not describe, nor the fondest love alleviate! How much rather would the mother lay herself down a victim, if she could but spare her beloved one!

And then to watch the death-struggle, and close the lids for ever over those eyes into which we have so loved to look! Oh, who can tell the anguish of the mother by the bedside of a dying child, but she who has experienced it? Does she not suffer as she walks, with drooping head and bleeding heart, through all "the earthly circumstance of woe" which follows in the path of the Death-Angel?

Yet all this is needed, for she, like "the great Captain of our salvation," must be "made perfect through suffering." The Christian mother treads in his bleeding footprints along the rugged but heavenward pathway. The time will come when every pang she has borne on earth will prove to have been the seed of an immortal joy.

IX.

LILLIE'S SICKNESS.

My babe lay sick upon my knee,
  And as I soothed its cry,
My heart went out in reverie, —
  "What if my child should die?"

Clad in the cerements of the grave,
  Should the dark angel come,
Could he my fair, sweet Lillie have,
  My darling, for the tomb?

And my poor heart grew pale and wild
  At thought of such a woe,
And closer still I drew my child,
  My cold lips answering, "No."

The tomb,—the damp, dark, icy tomb,—
  Oh, shadowy, fearful place!
To lay from out our pleasant home
  That precious baby face.

And the stern cloud of sudden night
  Had chilled my very breath;
When, lo! it parted to my sight,
  And showed me life for death.

He who that cherished bud had placed
  Upon this breast of mine,
Was bending o'er the form it graced,
  With sympathy divine.

I could not wonder he had sent
  To call again *his own*,
Ere all its sweetness should be spent,
  Its angel-freshness gone.

For earth is not a kindly place
  For rearing heavenly flowers;

They perish in our blind embrace ;
  They need their native bowers.

And when I knew that Love alone
  Would e'er recall the gift,
The darkness from the grave had gone,
  And death no sting had left.

X.

AN ANGEL CHILD.

I HAVE an angel babe, which awoke to its first consciousness in heaven, even before our eyes had beheld its earthly form. We buried the little body in the cold earth, and are waiting yet for our first vision and embrace of its pure spirit, which we are assured we shall meet, when our mortal shall have put on immortality. Say not it had no spirit, because disease, sparing the mother, fastened upon her offspring, and destroyed the tender life before it entered this earthly sphere. Had not my life given it form and structure, nourishment and vitality? Had not its spiritual nature, as well as its physical, for months been sustained by my own? Had not my daily dispositions and emotions made their impress upon its plastic organism? Had I not loved it with a love that made me forget pain, and cheerfully endure all sacrifice for its sake? And had not I prayed for it, and consecrated it to Him who holds me, and all I am, have, and hope to be, at his sovereign disposal? Had not his eyes of affection beheld this "substance, yet being imperfect, and written in his book," all its frail members, "which in continuance were fashioned"? And was all this for naught? Was the work of an almighty hand annihilated? We may reason and speculate about many things which we can not see or know, and our conjectures leave us as much in the dark as ever. But the intuitions of our spiritual nature who can resist? Intellect oftentimes increases our doubts, where feeling satisfies and assures us.

I *believe* that my babe *lives*, and that one day I shall see and possess her.

XI.

THE MOTHER'S OFFERING.

WITH a stricken heart and streaming eyes we bring our offering to the repository of the dead, the Mount Moriah of our earthly experience. We observe that the spreading fields are thickly sown with the slumbering forms of the little ones from many a household — the seeds of a glorified and immortal life. How closely are they laid, side by side, in their green, quiet resting-place. Oh, what loveliness, what symmetry and grace, what ravishing sweetness, is hidden from our sight, within the close confines of those little graves!

And here we lay our treasure.

> "The golden haired, the blue-eyed,
> That lighted up our life,"

we lay to sleep with the perfumed flowers, her tiny hands clasping the fragile bud, and the white blossoms entwined with her silky locks, all now alike faded. Oh, thou cold, inexorable grave! How much that is fair and beautiful has been torn from the warm clasp of love, to be given into thy silent and pulseless keeping!

But is it not *well?* Sad, drooping, suffering mother, shall we repine? Is it not a rare privilege to have an unsinning child to love and call our own, one who dwells in the immediate presence of the Infinite? Let us not grieve. Rather let us rejoice, smiling through our tears. Our ransomed little ones shall be a sweet connecting link between our souls and God; for surely if he makes our little ones his peculiar and pleasant care in his home above, he can not fail to cast a smile of recognition, of sympathy and tender love, down into the bereaved, weeping heart that has yielded up the gift.

XII.

THE DEATH OF A BABE.

Be still, my throbbing heart, nor ponder more
Upon the scenes of piercing sorrow past.
The languor, pain, the mortal strife are o'er;
My child is safe at last.

Her drooping head now lies on Jesus' breast,
Her beaming eyes look fondly up to his,
And those sweet lips, to ours so often pressed,
Breathe only health and peace.

Oh, had a language to her love been given
While here with us, what words would she have said!

What earnest thoughts for utterance have
striven! —
An utterance forbid.

But she has found a better speech above
Than earth could ever teach or compre-
hend;
Her unsealed lips to angel thoughts of love
Now sweetest accents lend.

Oh, had she lived, what various ills of life,
Vexation, sickness, grief, were hers in
store!
My fond heart feared for her the coming
strife;
But now I fear no more.

All, all is peace where she has gone to dwell,
And everlasting health, and joys com-
plete;
Her life, begun, flows onward, blissful, still,
Endless at Jesus' feet.

Yes, peace is hers for whom I dreaded strife,
And health, whose every pain was pain to me;
And joy, whose comfort was my dearest life,
My choicest ministry.

Then, shall I murmur? Shall I bid her come
E'en for that fond embrace I yearn to take?
No, darling! rest thee in thy better home.
My heart, it shall not break.

For Jesus binds it with his balm of love,
And thy sweet ministering touch I feel;
I soon shall join thee in thy home above:
All, all, my child, is well!

XIII.

THE MOTHER'S CALLING ONE OF LABOR.

THE mother is called of God *to labor.* Her work is an arduous one, untransferable, incessant, ofttimes perplexing and wearying. Many entertain the mistaken opinion that the possession of wealth excuses the mother from her peculiar work, and gives her the right, as well as the ability, to transfer her duties to other hands. But hers are duties which *can not* be delegated. *God* has made her the *mother* of the child, and, by this indissoluble bond of nature, has commissioned her to be its guardian and educator all the way up from infancy to manhood. She may not say, "The task is too hard; I have not energy sufficient to accomplish it. She must rouse herself to action, and seek supplies of strength and vigor from everlasting fountains. She may not think to excuse herself on the ground of unfitness. She must qualify herself for the part assigned to her — by the help of divine grace educating herself that she may educate her child. Unless God himself, in his holy providence, by any sad, unforeseen calamity, separates her from her offspring, thus taking her work out of her hands, she has no right to relinquish or forsake it. Money, social position, foreign philanthropic claims, however intrinsically important, confer upon her no privilege to neglect the watch and discipline of her little ones, or intrust them to other fashioning, molding hands. She may have helpers, as many as she finds it necessary or convenient to employ. Nurses may wait and tend upon weak and helpless infancy; seamstresses may be at hand to set the many-needed stitches; teachers, in every department of knowledge, may daily minister to the opening intellect. But the designing, directing, controlling hand, and watchful, loving eye of the mother must be always there, upon and over all. Hers must be a constant presence. Her example must be the hourly illustration of Bible principles and teachings, and furnish to the child a comprehensible model for every good habit, right motive, and generous affection. The management, the discipline, the entire moral training in the family must emanate from her. Her gentle voice must administer the remonstrances, reproofs, and exhortations; her tender hand inflict the necessary chastisement, or bestow the promised reward. If her course be a different one, does she not peril her own and her children's welfare.

No, the mother can not shake off her responsibilities. A necessity is laid upon her to execute her commission by the exercise of her own powers. The pastor, unfitted by circumstances to meet the duties of his vocation, employs a substitute, and transfers to him his work, his responsibility, his emoluments, and his final account. He is no longer the laborer in the vineyard, the steward of the household, the shepherd of the flock. The lawyer passes over his client to a brother professor, and is no longer answerable for any sentiment that may be uttered, or stratagem which may be employed. He is not applauded for success, admired for ability, or censured or commiserated for failure. The king who through imbecility allows his empire to be ruled by his chief minister, is not the monarch but in name. These may all, under the pressure of circumstances, give up their cares and duties into other hands, and no one will suffer by the change. Their respective labors may be carried forward even more skillfully than before. But the artist can never impart to another mind the ideal of beauty which his own has conceived, nor the taste, or skill, or genius, to bring out that ideal from the marble or the canvas. If that creation of his imagination is ever embodied, it must be by the patient labor of his own hands. So the mother is God's artist. In her hands is placed the material, to her is showed the pattern of the heavenly, upon her are bestowed the needed implements of labor, and *she* must fashion from perverse and wayward infancy the noble, godlike manhood. As long as her relation can not be annulled, her work can never be assigned to another.

Every mother, without doubt, wishes her children to be virtuous and happy. She talks well about it, and prays earnestly for it; but here the energy and zeal too often terminate. These are not strong enough to grapple with the difficulties, carry the crosses, thread a way through the perplexities that abound in a mother's pathway. She who would do well the work assigned her, must shake hands with discomforts and sacrifices innumerable. She is not found at the fashionable entertainment, for late evening hours will unfit her to rise betimes in the morning. She foregoes many social enjoyments lest they infringe upon that hallowed hour when her little ones go to their repose. Of all seasons in the day, at these two the mother and child should invariably meet. If she welcomes the bright, happy faces of her children, just awakened from their refreshing slumbers, with a pleasant good-morning smile, and superintends herself their toilet, she has a golden opportunity to gain the affections and impress the heart. She talks with them in simple manner of their duties and pleasures, their companions and temptations; instructs, encourages, and warns them. She plies them with holy motives, unvails before them the ever-present, loving Saviour, and so sends them forth into their little day-world, consciously engirded with her love, her counsels and entreaties, and the restraining presence of a watching and sin-hating God. Then, when the day draws to a close, and she bends over their couch, she talks with them of the occurrences of the day, of their sins, trials, and child-victories, and in the hallowing, subduing influence of that quiet hour, she has a power untold to win and bless them.

Aside from these special seasons, the mother should always know the whereabouts of her children, their companions and occupations. She can not watch them every moment, but, like a guardian angel, so hover about them that they can not be long in contact with evil but she shall know it and spring to the rescue. To her, as to a rock of refuge, they must be able to flee in all their little distresses and troubles, and her ear must ever be open to receive their confidence.

This constant watch, during the years of infancy, is necessary, in order that the mother may *herself* learn the character and detect the faults of her children. It is a commonly-received maxim, that parents are blind to the faults of their own children. The reverse of this ought to be true; for while a stranger would be repelled by their waywardness, the parental instincts and benevolence will overleap the sin and embrace the sinner. With a true Christ-like pity and compassion will the mother stoop to lift her child out of its errors and its sins into purity and right. And *no* fault should be suffered to pass unnoticed. It is not requisite that the child should be always spoken to at the moment, or before others. Nothing will discourage him more than incessant upbraiding, or a public notice of misconduct. More can be accomplished in correcting a bad habit by taking the transgressor alone, and mildly, but plainly, explaining the evil of his course, its unhappy consequences, and setting before him the opposite excellence. Such words in season will always do good.

A mother must be interested, too, in her child's studies as well as his sports, in his difficult exercises as in his amusements, and stand ever ready to cheer and help him. Instruction must be drawn from every occurrence of life, and motives, feelings, sentiments, words, and actions, brought up to the rigid standard of God's holy truth. To meet this unceasing demand, a mother must be ever on the alert. She must have constancy of purpose, stability of character, mental balance, sound judgment, firm principle. *Can she rest* while such a task lies before her yet incomplete?

Yes, mother, there is a rest. Fainting, wearied, perplexed, disheartened mother, weighed down by a sense of personal insufficiency, of stupendous responsibilities, fly to Jesus, the sympathizing Friend, and hide thyself in the shadow of his wings. "Virtue shall come out of him," to refresh and recreate thy weakness; and from this daily, hourly retreat, thou shalt come forth with heavenly strength and vigor to thy life labor, until, with its successful accomplishment, thou shalt receive the satisfying plaudit, "Well done, good and faithful servant; enter thou into the joy of thy Lord."

XIV.

HIRED LABOR.

WHAT hireling can fill a mother's place? Of low birth, in almost every respect untrained and ungoverned, without refinement, intellectual culture, or conscience, impulsive and selfish, regardless of the welfare of others unless it subserves their own advantage, destitute of Christian principle, and with ambition stimulated only by the lowest propensities, they come into our families to assist in the nurture of our little ones. The mother puts her babe into their hands; but the love implanted in her bosom in its behalf, for the very reason that *she needs* this most powerful of all prompters to make her its patient, tender, gentle, unwearying guardian and guide,—this holy *mother's love* she can not impart. Alas for the little ones doomed to grow up without it, unblessed by its warming, health-giving rays!

Neither can she transfer her knowledge, judgment, taste, refinement of mind and manners, her moral culture; and last, but not least, she can not pass over to her servant the sacred responsibilities which God put upon her when he placed that immortal spirit in her human keeping. She may suffer her hired help to perform every office of necessity and love for her child; to discover and deal as she pleases with his opening traits of disposition; to crush, for very want of knowledge, the buddings of good within him; to chide, threaten, tantalize, punish, deceive, bribe, and reward at the dictation of her own freaks and irritabilities; but who shall bear the curse of his manhood's crimes and vices?

The servant has trained the child, but her interest and care go no further than her salary; and she will neither care for his future virtues, nor blush and suffer for his misdeeds.

And who shall meet the final account? When the last great day shall come, and the mother and child shall stand together before the bar of God,—when the question is asked, "Have *you* trained this child for me?"—what shall she answer. Can she turn to the poor, untutored, illiterate menial at her side, and reply, "*She* trained the child, and I paid her wages: I had money to purchase ease and self-indulgence for myself, and I employed her as my substitute with my little one"? The poor girl who had done what she could, and as well as she knew how, may be excused on that dread occasion; but the mother—the negligent, ease-loving, pleasure-seeking, fashion-following mother—will never, through unending ages, be able to pronounce absolution on herself for her wicked indolence, her culpable neglect. She may, by virtue of her own trust in an atoning Saviour, find a place among the ransomed; and her son, through a personal accountability, be assigned for his sins to everlasting misery. Yet, as she sees the spirit, which she introduced into this immortal existence, sinking deeper and deeper in remediless woe, will she ever cease to cry, in the bitterness of her anguish, "Oh, my son, my son, would I had died for thee"?

XV.

THE MOTHER'S CALLING A STUDY.

THE mother needs to become a diligent student. Does the florist accomplish his work successfully without instruction, study, thought? Let him go into his garden or his greenhouse, utterly ignorant of the nature of plants, their habits and requirements, and he would inevitably injure or destroy, or at any rate would prevent the progress of, all he should attempt to rear. A few rough, sturdy roots might survive his rude treatment, but the tender plants would certainly die. And shall a parent go blindly to his work? Can a mother take hold of the precious plants of the Lord's house, — the delicate exotics of paradise, — and, without instruction or previous thought, train them aright? Surely here, if in no other department of life, "in the multitude of counselors there is safety;" and it is not only becoming, but an *absolute duty*, for a mother to avail herself of every means within her reach to increase her knowledge and her qualifications for her work.

With regard to the *physical education* alone, how many serious mistakes have been made through ignorance, affecting not only the health, but deteriorating the tone of both mind and morals in the whole after life! How many precious little ones have been laid away in the dark and silent tomb, who, but for these sad errors, might now have cheered the desolate fireside, and comforted the hearts of the bereaved and stricken parents! There are laws of nature, stern and unrelenting, which must be obeyed, or the penalty be endured. It is of no use to plead ignorance and good intentions. God, in his infinite mercy, may turn these calamities to our spiritual account; he may overrule them for good; but this does not remedy the fault, nor avert the punishment. Our only resource is, to learn all we can about these laws, and then strictly conform to them.

XVI.

THE CHILD-TEACHER.

"A woman lives
Not bettered, quickened toward the truth and good
Through being a mother?—then she's none, although
She damps her baby's cheeks by kissing them,
As we kill roses."

WHY did a God of love, and wisdom, and infinite resources give into woman's hands such a work of trust and responsibility? Because she was so pure, so perfect, that she was *qualified* to train his children for their eternal destiny? Was it not, rather, because in his prescient wisdom he saw that it would be a disciplinary and educating process for herself? Her child was to be the mirror in which she was to see herself; its relation to her to furnish the analogy of her relation to the good Father above; and by his ministrations of love, forbearance, tenderness, and sympathy toward her, she was to be taught how to love, and pity, and train those committed to her charge.

The parent was to be the acknowledged teacher of the child; but the child, also, was to be a teacher, silent and unacknowledged, save by the humble, simple, tractable spirit of the child-like mother. Ah, what an interplay of sweet educating influences is ordained of God between the mother and her child! Its involuntary instructions and constantly imposed restraints are to develop in her the simplicity, purity, and quietness of the subdued and Christ-like spirit. The daily self-denial is to her soul what muscular exercise is to the body: it gives vigor and strength to the system, flexibility and grace to every movement, and causes the heart-pulses to beat warmly and truly. Her round of duty is a book of study — deeper study than the dead languages or dry metaphysics, higher than poetry or the arts. She applies herself to find out her child, to learn its character, its disposition, its intellectual and moral organization; and as she looks down, down into the depths of its heart, and searches out its motives, its principles, its hidden springs of action, behold, she sees reflected there *herself*, with infirmities, defects, obliquities she had never dreamed of possessing. Now she applies herself, with diligent watch and prayer, to correct, reform, improve herself. Why? That she may furnish herself with the capability wherewith she may do the very same for her child. She learns that, to govern her child, she must first govern herself; to make him noble and magnanimous, she must be so herself; to infuse into him a hatred of falsehood and deceit, she must ever be true, artless, and sincere; to make him self-sacrificing, she must annihilate self; to teach him gentleness, she must put on the "meek and quiet spirit." In short, the mother *must be what she would have her child become.*

XVII.

WHERE SHALL I LEARN?

My dear M——:

You ask, "Where shall I acquire my new profession?"—an important inquiry, truly, in view of the holy relation into which you have just entered. Consecrate your little one to the Lord, I entreat you, at the onset, and yourself to the sacred work of training it for him. If my own experience can guide or help you, you are indeed welcome to it.

I gather every thing I can from books, for human instrumentalities are God's appointment. I consider money spent for extravagances of dress, for ornaments and glittering toys, as wasted; but money expended for books and lectures, and all the appliances of improvement, is a wise investment, and will bring a profitable return. Every thing that will make me a better mother I covet, and, as far as I can, procure. Nor are those books alone to be sought which are written expressly for mothers, enforcing moral obligations, and teaching the theory and practice of child-management. Practical scientific works are of incalculable value — such as, by giving correct knowledge of the material I am called to deal with, will teach me how to use and treat it.

I learn, too, all I can from my own and others' experience. My daily dealings with my children afford a text book ever open before me. If, upon trial, I find a course wholesome in its results, I follow it up; if inexpedient or fruitless, I abandon it, and try another. So I like, also, to go into other families, and observe the management of parents and children. The good I see I try to copy; the evil I learn to avoid and correct. I can observe evil and injudicious courses in others without crimination, for oftentimes they form a mirror by which I detect similar faults in myself. I can see excellences without a feeling of envy or jealousy, for they prompt me to immediate exertion to make those excellences my own. So, like the bee, which sips honey from every flower, extracting sweets from even the bitter and poisonous, it is the mother's privilege, with an eye ever observant, to extract good from the faults as well as the virtues of those who stand in the same relation.

The cultivation of *personal piety* will make me a better mother; therefore I must avail myself of every means of grace within my reach. "Bring me home something," said a smiling little girl to her mother, as she was preparing to go out to the weekly lecture. "I am going to lecture, my child, and what can I bring you?" "Oh, you will get the *good influence* there, mother, and that is better than any thing else." So, from every meeting, from the Bible, and from the closet, I ought ever to bring "the good influence" which shall help to mold the character of myself first, and then that of my children. As I become more like Christ, I shall see it more sweetly reflected from them. My temper will be milder, my manners more gentle, my words more affectionate, my whole course of life more consistent, so that I shall be to my child what Christ is to me —a living model for imitation. Or, rather, such purity will make me a transparent medium, through which the blessed Saviour may be seen so clearly, that his beauty shall charm, and the holy attraction draw the soul up to him.

XVIII.

WHAT IS EDUCATION?

EDUCATION is a comprehensive term. It does not, as very many suppose, mean alone intellectual culture, or that acquisition of knowledge usually attained in schools. It is the training of the whole complex being, — the physical, mental, moral powers, — toward some particular end. In one sense, our whole life is an educational season, in which Providence designs, by his various ministrations of mercy, discipline, and teaching, to fit us for the other life, the eternal, to which we are all hastening. In another and more common acceptation of the term, the period from infancy to manhood is styled the educational season, because in these early years we are to be fitted for the duties and events of mature life.

This education is accomplished, not in schools alone, or principally. The *home influence* is by far the most powerful in molding the character; then, the school, society, the church, nature, books, and daily surroundings; in short, every thing which is brought to bear, through the external senses, upon the mind and heart, educates. However transitory the impression, it does its part toward the formation of the character. As in the vegetable world,

> "Cold, heat, and moist, and dry,
> Do nurture and mature the grain,"

so, in the cultivation of a child's character, each joy and sorrow, duty, pleasure, and disappointment, has its formative power. From every passing event, however trivial, he draws up into his growing being that which shall finally develop his individual manhood.

A good education, such as every Christian parent *should wish* to give his child, implies a judicious regulation and application of all those influences and circumstances which help in the formation of a healthy body, a sound mind, and a worthy character. What discrimination, what caution, what wisdom does he need, to gather in these ten thousand influences, minute, obscure, ofttimes evanescent, and so to concentrate them upon the young life as to bring it up to the stature of the perfect man! Nor in this threefold work must one department wait for the receding footsteps of another. Such are the affiliations of our complex being, that all must begin and progress together. We can not, for instance, wait, as many suppose, for the perfection of the physical system, before we commence a course of mental training. If we do, the mind becomes so encumbered with weeds, and its powers so enervated by idle and roving habits, that it can never be systematically and thoroughly disciplined. Nor is it safe to wait until the child can understand reasoning and argument before we attempt to bring the moral nature into subordination. Else the will grown stubborn, and the selfishness rank, in the productive soil of a corrupt heart, will prove too strong for reason, advice, or discipline. No, the system from the beginning must be a complete system. For though at the very first the animal nature claims our more immediate attention, the little mind is very soon ready to receive its first infantile lesson, and the young heart opened to the influence of affection — its earliest, latest, best teacher.

There is *danger* of pressing the mind of a child, to the injury of its body, into an extraordinary advancement, and also of cramping the intellect by an unjust treatment of the moral faculties. But these extremes an intelligent and wise parent will always strive to avoid. The experienced florist knows how to attemper the heat, light, and moisture to his plants. He does not wish to force them through a precocious development to a premature decay. He makes the atmosphere genial — just such as to promote a healthy growth. His aim is, not to urge growth and efflorescence by artificial appliances, but, by shutting off adverse, chilling, noxious influences, and furnishing those which are kindly and truly wholesome, to encourage the natural expansion. Then the flower grows — and it can not help it — rapidly, symmetrically, luxuriantly. So with us. Our homes, like the conservatory of the florist, should be so arranged as to shut out, as far as possible, the heartlessness, the corruption, the miasm of the world, and to furnish and promote that cheerful, enlivening, nutritious atmosphere, which will cause our children to come up, as the Bible expresses it, "as willows by the watercourses."

XIX.

THE RIGHT BEGINNING.

THE wise mother will seek to understand enough of anatomy and physiology to enable her to treat the physical system of herself and her little one so as best to promote its growth, prevent disease, and insure long life, unencumbered by weakness and infirmity. And this, too, is a knowledge which needs to be brought into practical use *even before the birth of the child.* When Manoah earnestly inquired, "How shall we order the child, and how shall we do unto him?" the angel of the Lord replied by enforcing the directions which he had given to the mother on a former occasion. These seem to have been only the enjoining of a simple and strict physical regimen, as the means adapted to bring about the desired end — that of having a strong, well-developed, healthy child, fit to be used by the Lord in a special work. And might not many Samsons, both in physical and moral endowments, be born in this generation, if mothers understood and obeyed the laws of their being? We certainly do know of multiplied instances where the comfort and usefulness of an individual have been entirely prevented by hereditary disease or deformity, induced by the ignorance, carelessness, or willful wrong-doing of the mother.

XX.

CORRECT PHYSICAL EDUCATION.

THIS physical education is by a great many underrated. It is considered as a matter of course that the child will grow up according to its constitutional tendencies, and that attention to so many rules and principles will do no good, but will make the subject of them whimsical and fastidious. But as the tender sapling in our garden will not be likely to grow into a fine, symmetrical, noble tree without proper culture, so our children will not grow into a vigorous maturity unless the laws of the physical organization be duly regarded. We say *our children* — but our sons usually fare well enough, and our daughters are the unhappy victims of many and very fatal mistakes. We may say they have inherited disease, and therefore can never be strong and well; but it is a fact that many constitutions so tainted have been recovered, as it were re-created, by a careful regimen; and noble powers of body and mind have been rescued from the opening jaws of an early death, or from a lengthened vapid life, to the cause of God and humanity.

Many poor, suffering, worn-out mothers are full of complaints of their cross and fretful children — peevish by day, restless and wakeful at night. Others speak of the dull, lethargic intellect of their sons and daughters. "We fear they will never learn, never be fit for any thing in the world," they say. "But it is the sovereign dispensation of the Almighty, who in wisdom gives to one and withholds from another, and we must try to say, 'Thy will be done.' " Is there not a cause for these sad effects within the reach of the parents' eye and hand? Let the mother search and see, — like the skillful physician, let her examine the symptoms and ascertain the hidden root from which they spring, — and we venture to say that in ninety-nine cases out of a hundred she will find that the fault *is her own*, and lies in a direct and outrageous transgression of some plain law of our nature.

This subject is looked upon, moreover, as of the least importance in the training of a household, inasmuch as it does not take hold of the moral and eternal interests. But does it not? We are placed in this world to *work* — to advance the interests of the Redeemer's kingdom by active service. How can we do this, while our thoughts and time are absorbed in nursing a feeble and sickly body? If our bodies are the "temples of the Holy Ghost," does it not become a *religious duty* to make them pure, sound, and robust? A holy God would not accept that which was lame, deformed, or diseased upon the altar of his ancient people. Will he regard with any more approval the offering at our hands of bodies infirm, enervated, and depraved? We consecrate our children to the Lord, and ask him to take them, and use them in his service, and for his glory. Is there not danger that they may be spurned as a *worthless* sacrifice? Will not He who has said, "And if ye offer the blind for sacrifice, is it not evil? And if ye offer the lame and the sick, is it not evil? offer it now unto thy governor; will he be pleased with thee, or accept thy person?" — say unto us, as before unto his offending people, "I have no pleasure in you, neither will I accept an offering at your hand"?

XXI.

THE TRUE MODEL OF HOME.

God has given us the true model of home in his own most glorious abode, and ours must be as free in range, as sweet and relishful in its appointings, as radiant in the light of love, as heaven. We must be to our children what our heavenly Father is to us. Are we God's children? Then we know, or ought to know, how he bears himself toward us. He loves us through and through — not because we are lovely, but because he wishes us to become so. His love is not blind, but far-reaching and clear-sighted. He sees all our evil dispositions, notices every naughty and perverse way. He bears with our impertinences, turns not from our insincere repentings, wearies not with our repeated backslidings, and waits long and patiently for our love and obedience. He directs plainly, expostulates tenderly, trains steadily, chastens lovingly, mourns our delinquencies truly, and rejoices in our upward progress most earnestly. His love is a sun to warm us, a garment to envelop us, food to vitalize us. He appoints in this, our earthly dwelling place, the aliment to feed, the inspiration to awaken, the means to educate every upspringing faculty of our nature. Here are objects for our affections, work for our energies, food for our intellects, beauties for our tastes. No part of our organization must be left to wither out through neglect, to be choked by an undue growth of some other faculty — that all may be symmetrically grown, well-rounded, harmonious, perfect.

Here is our pattern. In this tender, affectionate spirit must we receive and train our children. With sound discrimination and sagacious judgment must we appoint the circumstances and surroundings of our families — by love begetting love; and the seed thus sown in faith and hope shall surely bring to us rich harvests of joy in the future. We are too circumscribed in our views, too short-sighted. We must consider beyond the present moment — look at the future bearings of present appliances, at the ultimatum of our labors. By and by our children are to be husbands and wives, fathers and mothers, in their turn. If we do not teach them the true idea of home, their firesides will one day echo back to ours their wailings and lamentations over disappointed hopes and crushed and withered joys. "O God, grant that my boy may never be such a husband as his father is! May there never be a poor heart to writhe under his torturing hand as mine now does beneath the anguish that presses it!" Such was the outcry of a poor, suffering wife, as she bent over the sleeping form of her only boy, and the burning tears of her heart-sorrow fell on his fair face. Then, young, earnest mother, begin the work in season. The rough, impetuous boyish nature must be polished and softened by the sweet amenities of home life, until his heart will vibrate to the most delicate, tender touch. He will lose nothing manly, vigorous, by it; and when he comes to have the tender, sensitive, confiding nature of woman in his keeping, he will be chary of his charge. Our sons should be encouraged to love music, pictures, birds, flowers, every thing that will gratify and cultivate the taste. They should also be taught all useful labors, with the feeling that it is never menial or degrading to bear a part of the daily family burden, for the sake of lightening the labors of those we love.

Our daughters, too, must be practiced in all household occupations, with the same feeling that every ministration for the aid or comfort of those whom we love is a labor worthy of celestial hands. It never demeans, but always elevates. Let the useful be well proportioned to the tasteful, the elegant, the decorative. All will harmonize within the inclosure of an affectionate, well-regulated home. To be able to get dinner, to sweep a room, to make a garment, to tend a babe, would add greatly to the list of a young lady's accomplishments. Where can we behold a more lovely sight than the eldest daughter of a family standing, in the sweet simplicity of her new womanhood, by the side of her toiling, careworn mother, to relieve and aid her? Now she presides at the table, now directs in the kitchen, now amuses the fretting babe, now diverts half a score of little folks in the library. She can assist her younger brothers in their sports, or the elder ones in their studies; read the newspaper to her weary father, or smooth the aching brow of her fevered mother. Always ready with a helping hand, and a cheerful smile for every emergency, she is as an angel of love and blessing to the home circle. Should she be called out of it to originate a home of her own, would she be any the less lovely or self-sacrificing?

This is the education which makes our children prize home; which will bind them fast around the family fireside; which will most effectually detain them from the fascinations and unprofitable gayeties of a corrupt and corrupting society.

XXII.

WHAT SHALL OUR CHILDREN STUDY?

WHAT shall our children study? is a question not at all difficult to answer, when applied to boys. The abilities of the child, the pecuniary means of the parent, or the vocation for which he is designed, will easily determine the amount of school education he is to receive. Schools of the first order are waiting for him, as soon as his parents judge him of sufficient age to enter upon systematic study. Here he is put through an elementary course, from which he may graduate into the classical school, from thence into college, and when the collegiate term is completed, all things being propitious, he can enter upon his professional studies, and crown the whole by a few years' travel and sojourn in foreign lands. There is no hurry. A young man has a plenty of time to furnish himself thoroughly for his prospective calling. Unless his money falls short of his outreaching desires, he may not stop in the acquisition of knowledge until all climes and countries, all people and languages, nature and art, the classics of ancient and modern type, science, history, philosophy, poetry, all have yielded their ample tribute to enrich his intellect, refine his tastes, polish his manners, and improve his manhood. Then he plants himself in his profession, and, if his moral culture has kept pace with his intellectual, he is prepared to acquit himself with honor and acceptance. All this is *well.*

And in order to prepare our daughters for the Master's use, their school education, too, *ought to be* thorough and complete.

There are good institutions, though comparatively few and unappreciated, springing up in various parts of our country, where young women, as well as young men, can be liberally educated. There let them be tasked and drilled, trained and disciplined, until their intellectual powers shall be drawn out, as the very word *educate* signifies. Let them go into the profound depths of metaphysics, the intricacies of mathematics, the vast mysteries of physical science. Let them dig through the opposing barriers of the dead languages for the hidden wealth of the ancients, and through the modern for the living literature of the present day. Be not limited by the erroneous notion that they will never need it. They *will need it.* Though they may never be pressed by necessity to put it to practical use by imparting it to other minds, yet they will need it. Education is not a mantle with which we may envelop our children, to enhance their beauty and attractiveness. Like the food they eat, it is incorporated into their very being; it is assimilated with their life; it becomes themselves; but themselves stronger, fuller, richer, more noble than they were before. It invigorates, vitalizes, fortifies the spirit. It makes the mind strong, yet elastic, so that, like the noble forest oak, which the tempestuous wind bends, but can not break, which yields to each driving gust, bowing its stately head, only to return with a natural grace to its usual uprightness, although it may meet and shiver under the sad concussions of a troublous and harassing life, still it breaks not, but returns from the pressure of sorrow and calamity with firm and cheerful bearing to its wonted course.

XXIII.

A RELIGIOUS EDUCATION.

WHAT is to be the *object* of a religious education? That our children may be saved. And from what? From the eternal wrath of God. But how can they be saved? By repentance and faith in the Lord Jesus Christ. They must "*become Christians.*" Now we can habituate them to all the external observances of religion. We can accustom them to daily prayer, the reading and study of the Bible, can send them punctually to church and Sabbath school, and rigidly enforce attention to every duty; yet, after all, we can not become Christians for them. This individual soul-work, dearly as we may love our children, we can not do for them. How then can it be accomplished? We must invoke the influences of the Holy Spirit, which alone can subdue and convert the soul. And will our prayer be answered? Yes, surely, for God has said, "Whatsoever ye shall ask, believing, ye shall receive." But *when* will the blessing come? How long shall we wait for it? Ah, this is the question so teeming with parental solicitudes. *When* shall the blessing come? And the answer sounds from every quarter, — an answer trying to our faith, because unsatisfying to our impatient eagerness, — "*When God pleases.*" And so we must wait, — alas, how many do it with a careless, easy indifference! — and, instead of working with all our might to help forward the desired end, we let our children come up pretty much as they will, with their selfishness unchanged, their will unbroken, their temper unrestrained, their pride uneradicated, with wrong habits of thought and action, growing firmer and stronger with every year, until at some future, uncertain day, when the Lord Almighty shall choose to come, and by some awful stroke of his divine power turn the soul suddenly and completely round into another course of inner and outer life.

To become converted is to be *reformed*— to become a "*new creature* in Christ Jesus"—to break up all the old channels of thought, feeling, purpose, and action, and to hew out new and opposite channels.

What a work! What a discouraging process! "Can the Ethiopian change his skin, or the leopard his spots? Then may ye also do good, that are accustomed to do evil." Is not this erroneous negligence the reason why there are so many "weak and sickly" ones in the church of Christ —so many mere "babes," whose age and intellectual attainments ought to constitute them "strong men" — so many decrepit professors, infirm in purpose, unstable in effort, serving in name under the banner of Emanuel, and yet the slaves of lust and passion, of appetite and sense, of self and the world? It is not in the range of possibility for a person to come up to mature years, habituated to a certain course of life, and then change right about and walk with firm, steadfast, undeviating progress in the opposite direction. He may, in the main, progress in the new life, but it will be with slow, uncertain tread, by fitful stages, with difficult and wearisome endeavors. "When he would do good, evil will be present with him." He will stumble, and rise, and fall again, in endless and disheartening succession. The insinuations of the world on the one hand, and the temptations of the adversary on the other, will sway him to this side and that, like a ship upon the boisterous and unsteady wave. He will be tossed to and fro upon the billows of selfishness, obstinacy, wrath, and envy, until he hardly knows where he stands, or whither his face is turned, and sometimes will sink in perplexity and despair, weighed down by the struggles, conflicts, and trials of his course. He will talk of the spiritual life as a warfare, and himself as a soldier beset with enemies, and often vanquished in the fight; and will represent to youthful beholders, that religion, though a necessary and desirable acquisition, is far from being an easy or pleasant one. Poor, wretched, starveling Christian! traveling along the King's highway of holiness, hardly bestead and hungry! Were it not for the matchless grace and tenderness of the kind and watchful Shepherd of the flock, scarcely would he reach the fold.

But must it be so? Must we and all our children be content to travel this hard and barren road, this "valley of Baca," all the way to heaven? No, thanks be to God, there is a more excellent way. Our little ones may be *trained up* in the way they *should go*, and when they are old they will not need to "depart from it." Let us begin in season, and by the grace of God assisting us, *form their characters so that they will never need to be reformed.* Let us take Christ for our model, and train in them every sentiment, opinion, impulse, and habit, to correspond with that heavenly pattern. Then they will grow up in the right direction, and when matured in understanding, will be prepared to live and labor for God. They will tread the pilgrim's path with a free and light, a swift and graceful step, unhindered by evil practices or unholy desires, and untemptable by the fascinations of a corrupting world. They will be indeed the "seed which the Lord hath blessed," a chosen generation, a royal priesthood, a holy nation, a peculiar people, prepared to be "witnesses for him" in the world.

XXIV.

DISTINCTION BETWEEN MORAL AND RELIGIOUS TRAINING.

THE *moral* and *religious* training of children, though producing similar results, yet spring from very diverse root principles. The one is founded upon the love of self, the other upon supreme love to God. The one is urged from considerations pertaining to this life alone, the other from motives drawn mainly from the life to come. The one aims at the approbation of erring, imperfect fellow-mortals, wins it, and travels on in security, admired and applauded, to the gates of the grave — but no further. The other "seeks the honor which cometh from God only," secures it, and walks on, hand in hand with the Divine, *through* the barriers of death to surpassing joys, honors, and rewards beyond.

There are parents who are rearing their families with the greatest care in all the proprieties, the moralities, the external nobilities of life, who inculcate every pure and virtuous principle, encourage each lovely affection and generous impulse, repress all growth of deforming wickedness. Their families are "pure, honest, lovely, and of good report;" but, after all, they are *without a God!* Such education takes no hold upon that other life, in comparison with which this is but as a hand's breadth. All the sweet amenities of our social and domestic nature may cluster richly about these prayerless households, and gild their passage to the inevitable tomb, but with a radiance which will not illuminate, but greatly enhance, the darkness of despair and soul-anguish which must succeed.

No moral training, how careful soever it may be, is sufficient. There must be deep, thorough, religious principle for its chief corner-stone and its crowning grace and beauty. God, the great Supreme, must be the glorious center, around which every thought, sentiment, and action should be taught to revolve. His holy Word, that revelation of his will and complete transcript of himself, should be the sure and solid basis upon which to build the superstructure of a symmetrical and perfect character. Our children, initiated by simple and easy lessons into the great mysteries of divine truth, must be led on carefully and steadily to the apprehension of the grand and all-embracing idea — that the "chief end of man is to glorify God, and to enjoy him for ever." Ah, stupendous, complicated teaching! How shall the infant minds of our little ones grasp that which so few, mature in years and in long profession of a Christian faith, understand? The religious training takes hold of far-reaching truths — climbs God-ward upon principles sublime and vast. How shall we, so untaught, so feeble, erring, blind, educe in our little ones that of which we know so little? May He who knows our weakness, and has promised to "lead the blind by the way they know not," who can bring order out of confusion, and overrule our very mistakes for good, help us in our laborious charge of leading the souls which he has given us upward to himself.

XXV.

EARLY CONVERSION OF CHILDREN.

DEAR M——:

No one can believe more fully than I do in the *certain conversion* of our children, *if the right method be used to bring it about.* The assurances of God on this point are as explicit as they can be, and, like all his other promises, "are yea and amen in Christ Jesus." Christ condescends to enter into covenant with his believing people, in behalf of their offspring, in the plainest terms. He pledges himself to grant his aid and crowning blessing, if we, on our part, will supply the correct and faithful training. *His* part of this covenant he stands ready *always to fulfill.* "The same, yesterday, to-day, and for ever," no change of circumstance can ever alter his purpose. If there is any failure, therefore, it must be on the part of the parent. The world, I think, has never produced an instance, and never will, of a child rightly trained going down to death. There are instances which, I know, *seem* to conflict with such a statement; but if the whole truth were known with regard to the home and parental influence in such instances, they would rather confirm than contradict it. Else, where is the foundation for our trust in the covenant and promises of the Almighty? If God sometimes fails to verify the assurances of his truth, what have we left to sustain our hope and faith? I might further say, it is my deliberate opinion that a child so trained will never come up into mature life a worthless member of society. Such is my sure confidence in a covenant-keeping God.

With regard to their *early* conversion, it is my conviction that it should be distinctly aimed at from the first years of the child's existence. Relying upon the influences of the Holy Spirit, which alone can regenerate the heart, we should diligently labor to bring truth before the mind, to present the highest motives of right conduct, to cultivate great tenderness of conscience, shedding around all the while the light of a holy example,—and while doing all this, *rest in Christ, waiting for this as we do for every other blessing*. Nor does this resting and waiting imply any cessation of desire, any indifference about the object. On the contrary, it promotes, as well as evinces, a calm, sure confidence, which nothing can shake, that the blessing will be given.

But the *time when* this saving change shall be wrought, whether in early childhood or more advanced youth, is the point around which, in my own experience, revolves the most thought, feeling, and solicitude. I know, as you say, that the command, "My son, give me thy heart," is an imperative one, demanding immediate obedience, and is as binding upon a child old enough to understand the requirements of the gospel, as upon a person of riper years. But this is an individual matter between Christ and the child. The parent stands and looks on, but can not do the work for the child, nor compel it done. Still he has an influence to exert. On the side of Christ, it is that of *fervent, persevering prayer*, drawn out by the assurance that "he will be inquired of by the house of Israel, to do this thing for them;" and by the promise, "Whatsoever ye shall ask in my name, I will do it." On the side of the child, this influence is that of *education.* As with older persons, so with the child; when this surrender of the heart is delayed, there is always something that hinders it. In some, it is pride; in others, obstinacy, or, it may be, want of resolution; or in some cases a love of, or earnest longing after, sinful or worldly pleasure.

It becomes, therefore, our duty carefully to study the character and disposition of our little ones, that we may find out where the hinderance lies. Then, with judicious management, we must seek, by instruction, example, and cultivation, so to develop the character as to meet and overcome the difficulty. That done, the child intelligently and immediately surrenders itself to the service of Christ. The time occupied by this preparatory process will be longer or shorter according to circumstances. The disposition of one child may be much harder to be met than that of another. It may also be retarded — and I think this is more frequently the case — by ignorance or want of care on the part of the parents. This oftener delays the work than a lack of prayer ; for how many pious parents there are who pray most earnestly for their children, — who go mourning all day long in great heaviness of heart on their account, — and who yet see them come up on the stage of active life sinful, and perhaps dissolute and depraved ! In such cases, the trouble is not with Christ ; nor is it originally with the child. The root of the evil is in them. They misunderstood the dispositions with which they were dealing, or mistook the means of correcting them ; or — more fatal error still — their own example, in some particulars, was radically wrong, thus continually giving the lie to their instructions.

Some parents appear to pray for the conversion of their children, as Elijah prayed for rain — expecting God, by miracle, to open the windows of heaven, and pour down the influences of the Spirit, to convict and convert the child, looking out all the while between their prayers, to see if the cloud is rising which shall harbinger the coming blessing. But it seems to me our prayers should be more like those of the husbandman praying for a plentiful harvest. *His whole life is an acted prayer*, while he tills the ground, sows the seed, and carefully nurtures the tender plant. He rejoices in the harvest in due season, though it is impossible for him to look back to the precise moment when the first tiny blade shot out of the ground. The blessing will come — whether at four, or eight, or twelve, or eighteen years, we can not foresee. But God's time will be the right time. The more intelligent and faithful we are in the performance of our duties, the sooner, I think, it will be brought about. The preparatory steps will be gradual, and more or less prompt, according to the disposition of the parent or child. The change, when it takes place, will be a momentary and voluntary one.

XXVI.

HOW SHALL WE LEAD OUR CHILDREN TO CHRIST?

We can not with safety lead them in a path which we have not trodden ourselves, for "if the blind lead the blind, both shall fall into the ditch." We can not instruct them in the true end of existence unless we rightly "apprehend that for which" we have been "apprehended of Christ Jesus." We can not bring Christ down to their infant capacity unless we are truly and intimately acquainted with him ourselves.

"Thy creatures wrong thee, O thou sovereign God!
Thou art not loved, because not understood."

Can we expect them to love one whom they know not? to seek to please one to whom they are totally indifferent? to wish to be like one who presents to them no attractions? *We* must then *live* at Jesus' feet. We must learn of him, and commune daily, hourly with him. He must be to us the "chiefest among ten thousand, and the one altogether lovely." He must be our choicest, dearest, most intimate friend — dwelling with us under our roof, associating with us in all our daily affairs. He must be our counselor in all perplexities, the sharer in all our joys, our comforter under all sorrows, the disposer of all our interests. All matters of opinions must be deferred to him; our judgments of persons and things all measured by his divine thought. We must speak of him freely and artlessly, as the child talks of its parent. We must run to him in every emergency, and rest in him with that confident, serene trust which the infant experiences in its mother's arms.

Can we have such a friend, and our children be uninterested? It is impossible. They will imbibe this affectionate, confiding spirit; acquire this habit of prompt and cheerful reference to "Him who is invisible," and manifest it in their budding experiences, as naturally as the waters of the tranquil lake unconsciously borrow the tint of the blue sky above. They will feel it to be a delight to gather with us at the Saviour's hallowed feet, and learn with us his holy teachings. Inspired by our confidence, they will begin to look up into his benignant face, and learn to watch the guiding motions of his eye. From that standpoint they will get correct views of truth and duty, of the deceitful ways of the world, the treacherous delights of sense, the insidious snares of the tempter. Here obedience, that principle of all others the most difficult to be ingrafted upon the child's corrupt nature, springs up and develops with fragrant luxuriance, displacing by its vigorous growth that perverse willfulness at which parental authority is for ever pulling and tugging, yet fails to pluck up by the roots. Love, too, from this glorious, ever-burning center, kindles and glows, and reaches outwardly, until the whole universe of God feels the radiance and warmth. Selfishness, the twin sister of a perverse will, melts away before the glowing of a heart full of Christ's love. Every thing wrong, sensual, hateful, unlovely, will now be avoided as soon as recognized; every thing right be carefully sought after. Duty becomes a pleasure, self-denial a privilege, prayer the soul's "vital breath," the Bible its treasury of uncounted wealth, the Sabbath a glad festival, and sacramental ordinances hallowed remembrancers of the dear departed, the unseen, yet ever-present Jesus. Every mercy will ring with the sweet music of his name, every sorrow be gilded with the radiance of his smile. Earth will seem but the continent across which we travel to meet our beloved, and heaven be welcomed as our home because it brings us to his blessed embrace.

If our children can be trained up thus at the feet of Jesus, is not the object of a religious education attained? Growing in such an atmosphere, will any thing else be needed to purify, soften, elevate—to round out the character? They will never know by experience "the gall of bitterness and the bonds of iniquity," or feel "the way of transgressors" to be "hard." But is it necessary that they should? Will it not be delightful for them in future years to look back and say, "We have never known the time when we did not love God, when the desire to please him was not the spring of all our conduct, when the wish to be like him was not our most cherished ambition"?

Will not children thus trained religiously, blessed by the judicious care of their parents with a healthful physical development, and well-cultivated intellects, make the right kind of material to build up our churches, repair the wastes of Zion, renovate and purify the world? Will they not be the fathers and mothers *needed* for the succeeding generation?

XXVII.

LABORERS FOR CHRIST'S VINEYARD.

Where and how are we to get men and women, of unflinching nature, divine intuitions, executive power, clear intellect, and loving spirit, who shall be co-workers with God in the renovation of the world? Where, fellow-parents, but from the fireside, from that school which God himself has incorporated, and over which he has commissioned us to be teachers? Do we know what is required of us? Do we realize the pressing need around us? Do we comprehend the mingled and overwhelming interests at stake? Do we understand the material we are set to fashion? Have we regulated *our own* power of action? Have we consecrated ourselves, body, soul, and spirit, in the name of God, to the work before us?

By what means, then, are we to achieve the desired end? We are convinced that it must be mainly by the *word of God* and *prayer.* If the Holy Bible is the infallible rule of our own faith and practice, and our children are taught with fidelity the letter and spirit of revealed truth, until to them, too, it has become the unfailing standard of right, the detecter of error, the inspirer of holy and potential motives, the medium of heavenly light, and the breath of love, —if we "pray always" with all prayer and supplication, and teach our families to commit every interest to God at a throne of grace, acknowledging him in all their ways, that he may direct their paths, — then we SHALL some day give to the world the unyielding Christian soldier, firmly battling for the right, the fearless expounder of truth, the practical, efficient laborer, the written epistles of God, known and read of all men, the unblenching witness for the pure and righteous Jehovah, the beautiful illustration of his glory, which is — how can it be any thing else but Love ?

Dear friends and Christian associates, let us all be wide awake to our duties. Let us not be induced by any power of selfish persuasion, or any temptation of the adversary, to remit our zeal or come down from our labor, for "the work is great." And may God help us, and give us *surely* the reward of our toil, that we may see our children growing up a seed to serve him — that the earth, which now groans and travails in pain under the pressure of sin and wrong, may be redeemed and filled with the glory of God as the waters fill the sea.

XXVIII.

THE TASK COMPLETED.

THE mother's work is never done, unless God takes it from her by a special providence, until her children are old enough to stand and act for themselves on the stage of mature life. From the birth of her eldest to the maturity of the youngest, she must work, work, work, watch, watch, watch, by day and by night, week in and week out, for months and years, following each other in long succession. We speak not here of material work; of the labor of the hands to supply the wants of the physical nature; the answering of, " What shall we eat, and what shall we drink, and wherewithal shall we be clothed?" Money can accomplish all this, if we have it; and if not, we will not sigh, nor fret, nor covet; for the heart-work, the solicitude of a good mother for a virtuous and honorable character in her children, walks forth with a bolder, steadier step by the side of frugality and daily labor, than it is apt to do if separated from them.

It is a well-known fact that almost all the true greatness, the noble virtues, the heroism which the world has seen, have arisen from the lap of obscurity, poverty, and toil. But the work to which we now refer is that which every mother, whether rich or poor, whatever the advantages or disadvantages of her circumstances may be, is required by the most sacred and rigid obligations to achieve — the assiduous cultivation of the inner nature, of that which makes the true man or woman, that which shall live for ever and ever. For this she must be always at her post, with never so much as a recess from her maternal care and solicitude, toiling on, breaking up the ground, sowing the seed, training the tender plant, enriching the soil, watering, nourishing, stimulating every good and pleasant growth, until the flowers begin to bloom, and the fruits to ripen. Then there comes a heyday of enjoyment, of rest and comfort to the mother, in the golden autumn of her life, when, surrounded by a group of affectionate, dutiful, virtuous, and noble sons and daughters, she sits among them in beautiful repose, her face radiant in the glow of her own heart's ever-burning love, and the smile of Heaven as a halo of light about her head — a spectacle to be admired and envied of all. But this season of comfort, this "Indian summer" of maternal life, never, *never* comes to those who evade their responsibilities, forsake their trust, and leave their work for others to do, for the sake of personal ease, sensuous indulgence, or selfish gratification. The very thing they seek, they lose by a lamentable and hopeless mistake, verifying the words of our Lord, "Whosoever will save his life shall lose it; but whosoever shall lose his life for my sake, the same shall save it."

XXIX.

TO A DAUGHTER JUST ENTERING WOMANHOOD.

Thou art going up life's way;
 I am going down:
The cross thou hast not lifted yet;
 I am near my crown.

Scarce hast thou tasted earthly joys;
 I have drank, yet thirst:
Nor grief nor sorrow stirs thy heart;
 Mine is nigh to burst.

Friends are thronging round thy path;
 Mine mostly are in heaven:
Love yet is in the bud for thee;
 Its fruit to me is given.

There's light and beauty on thy brow;
Mine is dull and sear:
Health, hope, and courage gird thee now;
I'm weary, weary here.

Life opens fair and bright to thee,
Like the sunny spring;
Heaven seems brighter far to me,
And earth is vanishing.

Soon I shall stand where angels sing,
Glad on yonder shore,
And fold my spirit's tiréd wing,
Resting evermore.

There I will wait for thee, my child,
Storing my heart's full love:
God guard and guide thee safely on,
Joining our lives above.

www.ingramcontent.com/pod-product-compliance
Lightning Source LLC
LaVergne TN
LVHW021416110826
845150LV00007B/1952

* 9 7 8 1 4 2 5 5 0 9 8 9 7 *